This book
belongs to

....

Other books by Mick Inkpen:
KIPPER
KIPPER'S TOYBOX
KIPPER'S BIRTHDAY
KIPPER'S BOOK OF COUNTING
KIPPER'S BOOK OF OPPOSITES
KIPPER'S BOOK OF WEATHER
ONE BEAR AT BEDTIME
THE BLUE BALLOON
THREADBEAR
BILLY'S BEETLE
PENGUIN SMALL
LULLABYHULLABALLOO!
WIBBLY PIG BOARD BOOKS
NOTHING

British Library Cataloguing in Publication Data

A catalogue record for this book is available
from the British Library

ISBN 0 340 63480 4

Copyright © Mick Inkpen 1994

The right of Mick Inkpen to be identified as the author
of this work has been asserted by him in accordance with
the Copyright, Designs and Patents Act 1988.

First published 1994
First paperback edition 1996
10 9 8 7 6 5 4 3

Published by Hodder Children's Books,
a division of Hodder Headline plc
338 Euston Road, London NW1 3BH

Printed in Italy by L.E.G.O., Vicenza

KIPPER'S BOOK OF
COLOURS
Mick Inkpen

Hodder
Children's
Books

a division of Hodder Headline plc

Red

Orange

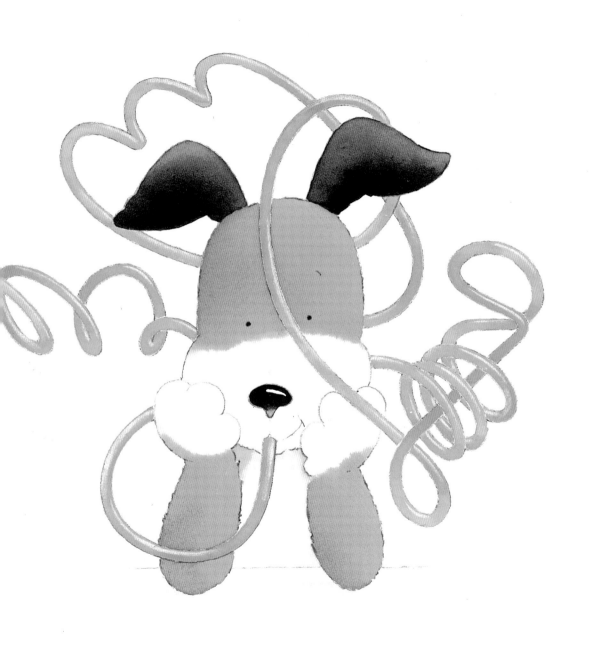

Purple

Green

Grey

Blue

White

Yellow

Black

Brown